D1643565

Wallace & Gromit

Weight loss with Wallace

Published by Ladybird Books Ltd
A Penguin Company
Penguin Books Ltd, 80 Strand,
London, WC2R 0RL, England
Penguin Books Australia Ltd,
Camberwell, Victoria, Australia
Penguin Group (NZ), cnr Airborne
and Rosedale Roads, Albany,
Auckland 1310, New Zealand

2 4 6 8 10 9 7 5 3 1

Ladybird and the device of a ladybird
are trademarks of Ladybird Books Ltd

Printed in China

Weight loss
with Wallace

AY-UP LAD!

Everyone knows that
I'm just crackers
about cheese,
but even I have
noticed that the
old waistline is not
quite as it used to be
(and my tank tops are,
tragically, a touch on
the tight side).

So, as ever, my faithful friend Gromit has come to the rescue by developing a programme of weight loss that's proved just the ticket. It includes a little of my favourite things (like cheese and the odd glass of bordeaux), a smattering of fruit and vegetables, and a light programme of gentle exercise.

So, best of luck, chuck – time to get cracking with the diet!

WALLACE'S FOOLPROOF WEIGHT LOSS FORMULA

Wallace's brain-altering device, the Mind-O-matic, could provide the perfect answer to your weight problem. However, for the less technologically-minded, there are other (slightly less dangerous) ways to change your eating habits...

FOR STARTERS

Write down your goal weight, and give all the reasons why you want to lose those extra pounds. You could also accompany this with a less-than-flattering photograph of yourself and place it on your fridge door or where you'll see it every day.

SERVICE

Name: Wallace
Target: Lose 20 lb
Reasons: Look better,
be more attractive to
women (or a certain
Lady); work without
losing me puff; keep
wearing my favourite
tank top.

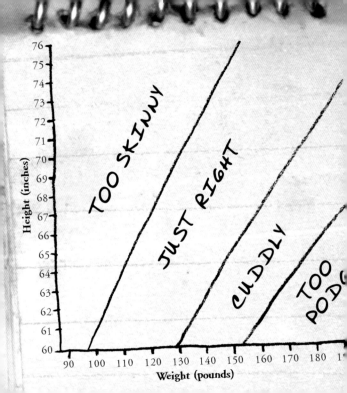

WHO ATE ALL THE CHEESE...

Wallace has drawn up a chart showing his ideal weight range. Find out your target by calculating your Body Mass Index (BMI) using this formula:

$$\frac{\text{Weight in kilos}}{(\text{Height in metres})^2}$$

BMI Result	Meaning
Under 18.5	Tank tops too baggy
18.5–24.9	Just the ticket
25–29.9	Tad too much gorgonzola
Over 30	Lock the fridge, Gromit!

GET DOWN THE GREENGROCERS

Stock up on healthy snacks; stave off hunger pangs by nibbling on a carrot or a nice juicy celery stick. Other options include: crackers with turkey breast, a banana, a small bunch of grapes, a glass of fruit juice, crackers with marmite.

Top Tips: 1

Keep a daily journal of everything you've eaten. It will enable you to keep a close eye on your food intake and can provide a real sense of achievement.

GIANT VEGETABLE COMPETITION

SILVER CARROT

AT TOTTINGTON HALL

FUN FAIR AND EN

5 days of propagation to go!

ONION CAULIES   ONLY 5ᴰ PER lb

WHAT, NO TREACLE TART?

Here follows a sample three-day diet, as devised and prepared by Gromit.

Day 1

Breakfast: Grapefruit compote and one slice of toast with marmalade; nice cup of tea

Lunch: Hawaiian crackers; nice cup of tea

Snack: Fun-size chocolate bar

Dinner: Turkey hot-pot, banana surprise (one banana); one glass of bordeaux

Day 2

Breakfast: Porridge with one teaspoon of jam; nice cup of tea

Lunch: Carrot soup; one slice of bread; nice cup of tea

Snack: Crackers with marmite

Dinner: Cheesy beans with crackers; melon surprise (half a melon); one glass of bordeaux

Day 3

Breakfast: Fruit and yoghurt swirl; nice cup of tea

Lunch: Fish fingers & salad; nice cup of tea

Snack: Carrots with cottage cheese and crackers

Dinner: Macaroni bake; rhubarb surprise (two sliced stalks with sweetener); one glass of bordeaux

'I'm just crackers about cheese.'
Wallace

Our Valued Clients

KEEP WATCHING THE PLATE

Eat slowly and try to focus on your food (rather than daydreams of romance) – it'll make you feel fuller and more satisfied.

WHO MOVED MY CHEESE?

If needed, remove temptation – banish all traces of Wensleydale or Gorgonzola from your house. Or put them somewhere really secure, like a crate in the basement.

Top Tips: 2

Try to remain focused on your weight loss. Remember there is more to life than a nice slice of extra-mature cheddar.

Cheese

MIDDLE AGE SPREAD

WATCH YOUR LOVE HANDLES

Alas, this can happen to anyone. The onset of middle-age brings with it a lower metabolism and a greater propensity for weight gain. **Result** – spare tyre and wobbly bits. **Answer** – exercise and keep a closer eye on your food intake. **Or**, learn to love your wobbly bits.

FANCY A BREW?

It's advisable to drink at least two litres of fluids a day when dieting. Water is the healthiest option although, thankfully, tea (sugarless with skimmed milk and WITHOUT chocolate digestives) is low in calories and can be consumed without guilt.

NO HONEST, THEY'RE NICE

Fresh vegetables
(preferably grown in
your own garden) are
a dieter's best friend.
Low in calories
and nutritious,
they're vital to any weight
loss programme. Pile
'em up and tuck in.

'Mmm,
lovely food
Gromit.
For rabbits,
that is...'
Wallace

COPING WITH CRAVINGS

Sometimes a little
bit of what you
fancy does you
good, particularly
if food cravings
becomes all-
consuming. But keep intake to a
minimum otherwise you'll ruin your
good intentions (and irritate fellow
housemates).

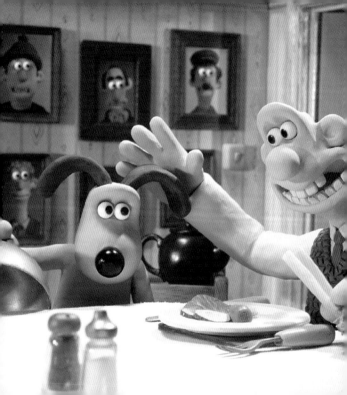

LOYAL FRIENDS

Ingenious mechanical aids are all very well, but it always helps to have a trusted companion on your side when dieting. They can offer invaluable support and encouragement at a time when willpower is a must. And, when needed, they can also chain up the fridge and lay mousetraps in the cheese box.

'Pile it up, lad. I'm in the moood for foood...'
Wallace

PUSH YOURSELF (GENTLY)

A programme of light exercise also helps to burn those extra calories, and is a cracking way to start the day. These exercises can be performed in the shed or parlour, and are suitable for dog or owner.

Starting position: Stand with paws shoulder-width apart. Keeping ears and tail pert, tilt pelvis upwards by pulling in tummy muscles and slightly rounding lower back, as you tuck buttocks under and feel lower back lengthen.

Inner-thigh stretching step 1:
Stand with paws shoulder-width apart and toes pointing outwards.

Step 2: Bend knees in line with paws until you feel a stretch in your inner thigh. Hold for 8 seconds and repeat.

Twists step 1: Stand with knees bent and over paws and a good pelvic tilt.

Step 2: Bend arms at elbow and with control, twist body from waist to right. Hold for a second and repeat to the left.

Arm circles step 1:
Bend knees and circle
arms down across in
front of body.

Step 2: As arms begin
to rise, extend legs
and rise up to toes
as arms reach above
head. Repeat slowly
eight times.

WHAT YOUR FEET ARE FOR

Think about whether you really need to take the van. Incorporating light exercise into your everyday life can really make all the difference, so how about walking to your next Anti-pesto job, or investing in a bicycle? You may need a box on the back to hold the rabbits, mind.

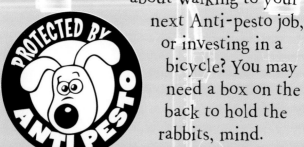

MAKE YOUR HEART BEAT FASTER

There's nothing like a little loving to spur on that diet regime. Those first tremblings of romance can stave off the heartiest of appetites (when the desire for food is overtaken by a yearning of quite different proportions).

DOING IT AT WORK

Keeping active at
work is an ideal way to
counteract excess cheese
consumption.
A morning of
strenuous rabbit-chasing
will soon work off even the
heartiest of breakfasts.

FANCY A LITLE NIBBLE?

Try to resist temptation when out for tea with friends, even when the tastiest of morsels are on offer. Although now and then one fairy cake won't hurt you!

Top Tips: 3

Breakfast is the most important meal of the day, and a much-loved ritual in the Wallace & Gromit household. Never be tempted to skip it as you'll be famished by lunchtime.

'Please Wallace - call me "Totty".'

Lady Tottington

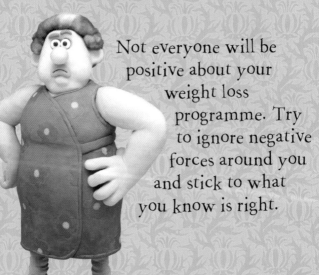

SOUNDS DAFT TO ME

Not everyone will be positive about your weight loss programme. Try to ignore negative forces around you and stick to what you know is right.

DO YOU WANT TO GO LARGE?

Not only are vegetables beautiful to behold, but they also make wonderfully nutritious snacks and are full of fibre goodness. And carrots the size of this one can keep you going all afternoon.

'I live for vegetables, they're almost a part of me.'
Lady Tottington

MESS WITH YOUR HEAD

If all else fails you could try a
mind-altering machine like the Mind-
O-matic. But remember, this is only
a LAST resort – mind manipulation is
a dangerous undertaking, only
suitable for those willing to
risk swapping their mental
abilities with
those of a
bunny rabbit.

'I do like
a bit of
Gorgonzola.'
Hutch

CHEESY CALORIE COUNTER

Cheese per 28g (1oz)	Calories	Fat
Brie	88	7.0
Camembert	88	7.0
Cheddar	120	9.8
Cottage Cheese	27	1.2
Dolcelatte	100	8.0
Edam	90	7.0
Emmenthal	115	8.0
Feta	85	7.0
Gorgonzola	94	7.6
Parmesan	118	9.8
Red Leicester	112	9.4
Roquefort	88	7.5
Wensleydale	103	8.7
Cracker (each one)	34	1.2